ALKALINE DIET

Ultimate Guide for Beginners with Healthy Recipes and Kick-Start Meal Plans

Emma Green

Copyright © 2018 by Emma Green.

All rights reserved.

No part of this book may be reproduced in any form or by any electronic or mechanical means – except in the case of brief quotation embodied in articles or reviews – without written permission from its publisher.

Disclaimer

The recipes and information in this book are provided for educational purposes only. Please always consult a licensed professional before making changes to your lifestyle or diet. The author and/or publisher shall have neither liability nor responsibility to anyone with respect to any loss or damage caused or alleged to be caused directly or indirectly by the information contained in this book. All trademarks and brands within this book are for clarifying purposes only and are owned by the owners themselves, not affiliated with this document.

Images from shutterstock.com

CONTENTS

INTRODUCTION 6

CHAPTER 1. The Basics 7
- What is the Alkaline Diet 7
- Guiding Principles of the Alkaline Diet 9
- What to Eat and What to Avoid on the Alkaline Diet 13
- Getting Started 16

CHAPTER 2. 3-Week Alkaline Meal Plan 17

CHAPTER 3. Recipes 21

BREAKFAST 21
- Good Morning Popeye 21
- Garden Pancakes 22
- Tropical Granola 23
- Summer Fruit Salad with Lime & Mint 24
- Winter Fruit Compote with Figs & Ginger 25
- All-American Apple Pie 26
- Baby Potato Home Fries 27
- Breakfast Fajitas 28
- Brown Rice Porridge 29
- Spaghetti Squash Hash Browns 30

SALADS 31
- Salad in Your Hand 31
- Warm Spinach Salad 32
- Salad on a Stick 33
- Emeraland Forest Salad 34
- Summer Dinner Salad 35
- Roasted Vegetable Salad 36
- Quinoa & Avocado Salad 37
- Avocado-Caprese Salad 38
- Spicy Sesame Noodle Salad 39
- Organic Baby Tomato & Kale Salad 40

BOWLS 41
- The Asian Bowl 41
- The Breakup Bowl 42
- The Fight It Off Bowl 43
- The Hawaiian Bowl 44
- The Indian Bowl 45
- The Italian Bowl 46
- The Mexican Bowl 47
- The Rose Bowl 48
- The Southern Bowl 49

MAIN DISHES 50
- Better than Chicken Soup 50

Angel Hair Pasta with Tomato Sause	51
Stuffed Peppers	52
Curried Eggplant	53
Championship Chili	54
Date Night Broccoli Bake	55
Thanksgiving Anytime Roasted Vegetables	56
BBB Soup	57
Grilled Vegetables Stack	58
No BS Brussels Sprouts	59
Sprouted Beans	60

DESSERTS 61

Coconut Ice Cream Sundae	61
Warm Peach Cobbler	62
Thanksgiving Pudding	63
Valentine's Day Dates	64
Melon Madness	65
Summer Fruit Crisp	66
Summer Afternoon Ice Pops	67
No-Bake Fig Newtons	68

SMOOTHIES 69

Tropical Pina Colada Smoothie	69
Banana Nut Bread Smoothie	70
Orange Healthy Smoothie	71
Mango, Papaya, Raspberry Smoothie	72
Pumpkin Drink	73
Basic Green Smoothie	74
More-Than-a-Mojito Smoothie	75
Avocado & Spinach Smoothie	76
Orange, Peach, Kale Smoothie	77

CONDIMENTS, SAUCES & DRESSINGS 78

Homemade Ketchup	78
Salsa Fresca	79
Hawaiian Salsa	80
Great Gravy	81
Apple Butter	82
Sun-Dried Tomato Sauce	83
Enchilada Sauce	84

CONCLUSION 85

Recipe Index 86

Conversion Tables 87

Other Books by Emma Green 88

INTRODUCTION

An alkaline diet is a holistic approach to health and well-being. It is a set of simple but very effective diet and lifestyle principles that will give your digestive system balance and get your body back to its naturally healthy state.

How often do you eat quickly, on the run, or late in the evening? And how often do you feel tired, lacking in energy, and have a gassy, bloated stomach? These are sure signs your body is suffering from too much acid. The alkaline diet is the solution. It will recharge you and reset your metabolism so that you can enjoy the energy levels you used to.

The benefits of the diet are both marked and swift. Regardless of your age and general level of health, if you follow the principles and the 3-week meal plan in this book, you will begin to see results within two weeks.

The diet is a powerful anti-aging program that will transform you from the inside out. The first benefits tend to be weight loss, increased vitality, and improved complexion, skin tone, and hair luster—which is why it is often called a beauty cure. It will also reward you with stronger bones, better moods, enhanced brain function, and a stronger immune system.

The alkaline diet is not a weight-loss program, although that may be one of its most popular benefits. We can achieve that by cleaning our system of toxins and identifying the foods and habits that will help us perform better.

CHAPTER 1. The Basics

What is the Alkaline Diet

The human body handles a carefully regulated pH balance by eliminating excess acid. The Standard American Diet involves mainly things like white flour, animal products, sugar, and alcohol. Our bodies can maintain a certain amount of these foods, but when we eat a lot of acidifying items and don't eat enough of the foods that support our body's ability to neutralize the acid, we become imbalanced. The body is, at times, unable to decrease excess acid in order to maintain an optimal balance. Some scientists believe that it's this imbalance that leads to various illnesses and diseases.

An alkaline diet involves foods that promote alkalinity in the blood and urine. These foods include fruits, vegetables, and certain whole grains. This diet balances acidifying foods and alkalizing foods so that the body functions more effectively.

In chemistry, the pH scale is used to determine whether water-based mixtures are acidic, basic, or neutral. The pH scale, ranging from 0 to 14, measures how acidic or basic a substance is.

- A pH of 7 is neutral.
- A pH less than 7 is acidic.
- A pH greater than 7 is alkaline.

Some foods included in the alkaline diet may have an acidic pH (like lemons), but have an alkalizing effect on the body. So, you can't simply determine whether to eat a certain food just by looking at its pH level. But the result of Western world eating habits is that the urine can become slightly too acidic, which indicates an overload of acid. Not enough to kill us, but enough to cause an imbalance that can lead to disease.

This happens as a result of foods that are too high in fat, protein, and sugars. When your body breaks down these foods, acid by-products form. As you might remember from high school chemistry—or from popping antacids when you feel heartburn—the way to neutralize acid is to combine it with a base. So, to reduce the acid burden, your body uses alkaline minerals to link to the excess acid so the body can eliminate the acid. In a healthy person, the system works to keep the body in a slightly alkaline range (a pH of 7.35 to 7.45). If your diet is very imbalanced, with too much acid and not enough alkalizing minerals, the body can't eliminate the acid by-products. They build up in the cells of your organs and reduce the efficiency and effectiveness of your body's function.

It's not just the foods we eat. Pollution, viruses, bacteria, and health problems add extra strain on our bodies. To combat physical stressors, the body releases stress hormones, such as cortisol, adrenaline, and insulin. Your body reacts by slowing digestion. The result is that the food you eat sits longer in your stomach and isn't digested well. So, your body doesn't obtain the optimum amount of nutrients from the food to help it rebuild and repair.

Eating too much acid-producing food wreaks real havoc on your entire body. It has to work harder to maintain a healthy pH balance. The alkaline diet works in two ways:

- ✓ It eliminates foods that have an acidifying effect on your body.
- ✓ It adds nutrients that help repair your body.

Numerous studies revealed that the alkaline diet resulted in a number of health benefits, some of which include:

- ✓ The increased amounts of fruits and vegetables improve the body's potassium-sodium ratio. This may benefit bone health and muscle tone, and lessen chronic illnesses like hypertension.
- ✓ An alkaline diet can help slow the natural loss of muscle mass that comes with aging.
- ✓ Many alkaline foods are rich in magnesium, a mineral that activates vitamin D, which benefits our bones, kidneys, and hearts, among other things.
- ✓ If you're recovering from an illness or chronic condition, the alkaline diet will infuse your body with much-needed nutrition to start the healing process, and it removes the additional stressors that a bad diet can create.

Guiding Principles of the Alkaline Diet

The alkaline diet is a prescription for health designed to help pull your body out of its acidic state by balancing your acid/alkaline intake. It's important to pay attention to how you're eating and how you feel afterward. Do you rush meals so you can move on to something else? Do you wash your food down with a drink during a meal? Do you only chew a few times and then swallow food almost whole? All of these have a bigger impact on your overall health than you realize.

Eating alkaline means breaking away from some of the accepted norms that you've grown accustomed to, particularly when it comes to portion size. To reap the long-term benefits of the diet, take into account to the ten principles of the alkaline diet as the way to harmony and balance, not just in nutrition but in life.

- ✓ **Be mindful**

Balancing your body and your mind should start with awareness of how your body feels, how you respond emotionally to situations, and your eating and lifestyle habits. It is about centering yourself, knowing yourself, and being in calm control of yourself.

Many of us have come to view meals as a necessity that can be bashed out of the way to make time for doing other things, such as work, house chores, or television. Mealtimes should be our own time, family time, a chance to anchor and be at one with the world. Considering how important food is to keep us alive, we should give it more of our time. When we don't do that, we diminish our spirit, our nutrition. We won't always have time to do this, but erring toward this as often as possible is highly beneficial.

Five steps for mindful eating:

1. Give yourself time to eat. Each meal time should take no less than thirty minutes.
2. Make sure you are comfortably seated. Be thankful that you have nutritious food to eat.
3. Notice any feelings of impatience and urges. Perhaps you are thinking of things you need to do, but try to concentrate. This time is dedicated to enjoying your food.
4. Chew thoroughly, around thirty times is the minimum. Think about how much food you put on your fork—the smaller, the better. Smell your food—breathe in the mouthwatering aromas.
5. When you have finished, stay seated and relaxed for a few minutes. You should feel calm, satisfied, and nourished, not bloated or overfull.

- ✓ **How to eat**

The first law of eating well is to take your time. Do not eat when you are stressed or angry, which might cause you to hurry. When you do eat, it's important to set aside enough time to give your body a chance to absorb what it is being fed, especially at breakfast and lunch. You need to relearn the pleasures of eating properly.

Your body digests different foods in different parts of the digestive tract and needs time to carry out this process. Your body will perform this task more efficiently when you are relaxed.

- ✓ **What to eat**

What you eat directly affects your alkaline/acid balance. The ideal alkaline to acid ratio is 2:1—meaning every acidic food should be paired with twice the amount of alkaline foods.

However, it's not just the type of food that you eat but also the quality of your food that has a significant impact on your health. The mineral profiles of vegetables are affected by factors such as the soil they are grown in since that is where the vegetables themselves source their nutrition. Therefore, you should look for fresh, seasonal, local foods of the best quality to make sure that what you eat is worthwhile both gastronomically and nutritionally. Organic produce is generally better because if your food is grown using pesticides and fertilizers, it is going to be nutritionally depleted.

Food always has more value when it comes from the land and sea around you. The greater the distance it has come, the more hands that will have touched it, and the more likely that it will have been processed or acidified along the way.

✓ **When to eat**

Breakfast and lunch should be the most important meals of the day. When you wake in the morning, your body is at its most able, in a digestive sense. It can cope with a wide range of different foods more easily. In the evening, your body is slowing down, so you are looking for smaller portions of more digestible foods. The habit of eating substantial meals later in the evening is not good from a digestive point of a view. Evening meals should be consumed early, preferably before six in the evening, since eating late can disrupt the body's rhythm. Your body starts to slow down after sunset, preparing for sleep at nightfall. During sleep, your body and your digestive system need a break to cleanse and prepare for the next day. If you eat a meal as your body is winding down in the evening, then your metabolism is forced to gear up to digest the food, using energy while you sleep. This activity can result in poor sleep and lethargy.

✓ **How much to eat**

Most of us eat too much—more than we need, more than our bodies are designed to cope with, and more than our bodies need nutritionally. If your diet is varied enough to include a complete spectrum of vitamins, minerals, and amino acids, then we don't actually have to eat that much.

If you tend to eat meals that are two, three, or sometimes four times larger than our stomachs, your body has to pump more and more energy into digesting the unusually large load. This leads to exhaustion of your body's systems, leaving you physically and mentally lacking in energy.

Changing portion size is an easy way to reduce your intake. You can try using smaller plates to eat off of, or a teaspoon rather than a tablespoon. Make every mouthful count and enjoy eating.

- ✓ **Stay hydrated**

Water is a crucial component of an alkaline diet. It helps clean the body and keeps us hydrated. You should start drinking it early in the morning and also develop a taste and respect for it. Drinking water helps circulate nutrients around the body and flushes out toxins. Keeping hydrated also has a positive effect on our skin. Given how important it is, it is worth taking more seriously.

You have to drink at least half a gallon of water a day. Plain water is the best, but liquids easily combine, so teas can contribute to your intake.

However, drinking while eating is not recommended because it dilutes your valuable saliva and stomach acid. Drink approximately half an hour before or after meals. If you have water at the table, the temptation is to wash your food down your throat. Water is valuable but not at the same time as food. There is drinking time, and there is eating time.

- ✓ **Exercise regularly**

Exercise promotes weight loss, strengthens muscles, improves blood flow, and stimulates the brain to produce dopamine—a hormone known to lift the mood.

The stronger you are physically, the better you support your digestive system. Regular exercise does not have to be hard to be beneficial. Walking is a natural motion; running long distances perhaps less so. Body movements that shift your frame, your stomach, and your chest are a part of keeping supple and toned. You should aim for a minimum of thirty minutes of deliberate cardio exercise every day—walk to work, bike, or take the stairs instead of the elevator. Some simple stretching exercises are good, too.

Be realistic and mindful of your current health status. Exercise in moderation. This is not a competition; it is about you and making you feel better. It is a regular routine of steady body movement that will deliver the important results. Routine is the key word here but avoids repetition. Combine the types of exercise you do and the parts of your body that you focus on. The point of exercise is to keep our bodies functioning through their easy, natural rhythms that support our natural shape.

- ✓ **Enrich your surroundings**

How we live is also a reminder of how we are setting out to cleanse and improve our inner health. A few visible, everyday symbols are worth acquiring: candles, calming music, a new water jug and glass. Simple things that help mark your progress.

Your home environment has a significant impact on your health and well-being. Even if you live in an inner-city apartment, making a few changes to your home can bring enormous benefits:

- Buy some fresh flowers and plants for each room. They remind us of nature, remove toxins from the air, and produce oxygen.
- Open the windows to improve airflow.
- Play pleasurable music—either to energize or relax you.

- Turn off computers and electrical devices in the bedrooms when not in use, but especially when sleeping at night. Appliance lights can stimulate your senses and prevent full, deep sleep. Some also believe that overexposure to the radiation from electrical devices can impact your health.

✓ **Find your rhythm**

Life is rhythms and cycles. Day. Night. Summer. Winter. Our bodies are a part of these natural cycles. Sometimes we have to remind ourselves that these changes are good—even a harsh winter after summer purges the ground as well as our souls. We work hard, we rest, we sleep, we are renewed, and we start again. These rhythms and cycles are essential to our well-being. Not following these natural cycles would be turning ourselves into mechanical clockwork machines.

We are not machines, but we sometimes drive ourselves like we are. Of course, it is admirable to work long hours and to push ourselves and to achieve. But once we have achieved what we set out to do, we must allow our bodies time to recuperate. We need to find the off switch and turn off the engine. It is not lazy to break off and take time out. It is necessary.

Routines break the day and will give you back a sense of purpose. Have a glass of warm water when you wake up. Start the day with a skin brush and morning shower. Open the windows and try some stretching. Go for a short walk to breathe the air outside and then have breakfast.

With the increasing speed and intensity of modern living, rest is as important as work—even a nap in the afternoon can be a good thing. You must realize that you cannot keep doing everything all the time. Try to interrupt your working routine every ninety minutes or so. Ideally, you should operate on ninety-minute cycles—seventy-five minutes of concentration and fifteen minutes of rest and recuperation. This time should be a deliberate intervention. Open a window or go for a stroll. And be sure to make time for lunch—thirty minutes' eating time at least. Remember to mix up your restorative activities.

What to Eat and What to Avoid on the Alkaline Diet

Acid-Forming Foods to Avoid

On the alkaline diet, you'll want to avoid animal products (meat, dairy, fish, and eggs). Also avoid alcohol, coffee, and black tea, as they are highly acidic. Similarly, refined sugars of any kind should be avoided. And, as most grains have an acidifying effect on the body, they should be avoided, too.

Here is a more extensive list of acid-forming foods to avoid.

Beans, Legumes, and Milks

- Rice milk
- Soy beans
- Soy milk
- Unsprouted beans

Fats and Oils

- Avocado oil
- Butter
- Canola oil
- Corn oil
- Flax oil
- Hemp oil
- Lard
- Olive oil
- Safflower oil
- Sunflower oil
- Acidifying Fruits
- Blueberries
- Canned or glazed fruits
- Cranberries
- Currants

Grains and Grain Products

- Amaranth
- Barley
- Bran, oat
- Bran, wheat
- Bread
- Corn
- Cornstarch
- Crackers, soda
- Flour, wheat
- Flour, white
- Hemp seed flour
- Kamut
- Noodles
- Oatmeal
- Oats, rolled
- Pasta
- Rice cakes
- Rice, white
- Rye
- Spelt
- Wheat
- Wheat germ

Nuts and Butters

- Cashews
- Legumes
- Peanut butter
- Peanuts
- Pecans
- Tahini
- Walnuts

Sweeteners

- Carob
- Corn syrup
- Sugar

Vegetables

- Corn
- Lentils
- Olives
- All Alcohol
- Beer
- Hard liquor
- Spirits
- Wine
- All Animal Protein
- Beef

- Eggs
- Fish
- Lamb
- Organ meats
- Pork
- Poultry
- Rabbit
- Sausage
- Shellfish
- Venison
- Dairy
- Butter
- Cheese, processed
- Ice cream
- Yogurt

Other

- Black tea
- Cocoa
- Coffee
- Ketchup
- Mustard
- Pepper
- Soft drinks
- Vinegar

Alkaline Foods to Enjoy

Fruits

- Apple
- Apricot
- Avocado
- Banana
- Berries
- Blackberries
- Cantaloupe
- Cherry, sour
- Coconut, fresh
- Currant
- Date, dried
- Fig, dried
- Grape
- Grapefruit
- Honeydew melon
- Lemon
- Lime
- Muskmelon
- Nectarine
- Orange
- Peach
- Pear
- Pineapple
- Raisins
- Raspberry
- Rhubarb
- Strawberry
- Tangerine
- Tomato
- Tropical fruits
- Umeboshi plum
- Watermelon

Proteins

- Almond
- Chestnut
- Millet
- Tempeh, fermented
- Tofu, fermented
- Whey protein powder

Seasonings and Spices

- Chili pepper
- Cinnamon
- Curry
- Ginger
- Herbs, all

- Miso
- Mustard
- Sea salt
- Tamari

Sweeteners

- Stevia

Vegetables

- Alfalfa
- Barley grass
- Beet greens
- Beets
- Broccoli
- Cabbage
- Carrot
- Cauliflower
- Celery
- Chard greens
- Chlorella
- Collard greens
- Cucumber
- Daikon
- Dandelion
- Dandelion root
- Dulce
- Edible flowers
- Eggplant
- Fermented vegetables
- Garlic
- Green beans
- Green peas
- Kale
- Kohlrabi
- Kombu
- Lettuce
- Maitake
- Mushroom
- Mustard greens
- Nori
- Onions
- Parsnip
- Pea
- Pepper
- Pumpkin
- Radish
- Reishi
- Rutabaga
- Sea vegetables
- Shiitake
- Spinach, green
- Spirulina
- Sprouts
- Sweet potato
- Tomato
- Wakame
- Watercress
- Wheat grass
- Wild greens

Other

- Apple cider vinegar
- Bee pollen
- Fresh fruit juice
- Green juices
- Lecithin granules
- Molasses, blackstrap
- Probiotic cultures
- Soured dairy products
- Vegetable juices
- Water, alkaline antioxidant
- Water, mineral

Getting Started

The best time to start the alkaline diet is on a weekend or a day when you are not going to be distracted so you can give yourself enough time to get organized. Keep things simple and straightforward and do what is manageable for your schedule. If you prepare your breakfast the night before, you will have all the elements easily on hand without having to think about it in the morning. Also, if you make up your vegetable tea or soup the night before, it will have time to infuse properly.

Depending on how acidic your body is, you will likely feel some side effects as you go: headaches, fatigue, anxiety, mood changes, or cravings. These are good signs, signs that your body is getting rid of toxins. They will pass quickly enough. Remember that many of our health problems have built up over several years, and real change may take time. The next fourteen days is a start.

The week before you start

You might reward yourself with a couple of days of vacation from work to get you up and going. Pencil a date on your calendar and give yourself a few days to get used to the idea. It is also good to adopt a few new changes before starting the alkaline diet:

- Cut down on a few small things like coffee, alcohol, and carbonated drinks.
- Don't buy any fast food, junk food, or packaged food, and clean out your refrigerator and pantry so you are not tempted.
- Cut out sugar, especially refined sugar.
- Start drinking water and get into the habit of drinking half a gallon (two liters) or more a day.
- Get your shopping list together for the first few days so you have everything on hand at home. Do not be tempted to economize on your shopping—the best, freshest produce will create the tastiest, healthiest recipes. Your food portions over the next two weeks will be fairly controlled, so you should be able to afford to be a little extravagant with the quality of your groceries.
- Use smaller plates. Plate your meals on side plates or in bowls rather than on big dinner plates.
- Start establishing a relaxing new evening routine. For instance, take a walk after dinner and give yourself some personal time to listen to music or read a book. Two hours before bed, take a warm bath.

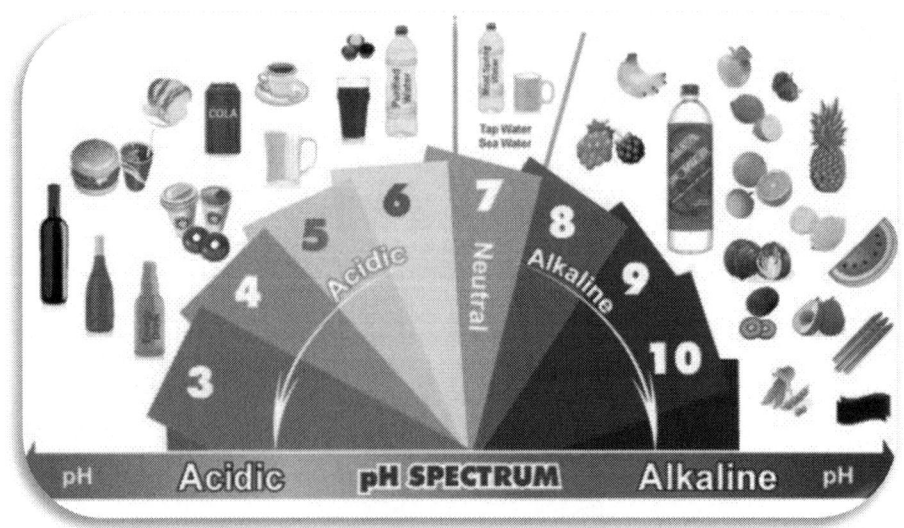

CHAPTER 2. 3-Week Alkaline Meal Plan

Week 1

	Wake up	Breakfast	Lunch	Dinner
Sunday	Banana Nut Bread Smoothie (recipe p.70)	Garden Pancakes (recipe p.22)	Avocado-Caprese Salad (recipe p.38)	Grilled Vegetables Stack (recipe p.58)
Monday	More-Than-a-Mojito Smoothie (recipe p.75)	Baby Potato Home Fries (recipe p. 27)	Salad on a Stick (recipe p.33)	Stuffed Peppers (recipe p.52)
Tuesday	Tropical Pina Colada Smoothie (recipe p.69)	Good Morning Popeye (recipe p.21)	Warm Spinach Salad (recipe p.32)	The Asian Bowl (recipe p.41)
Wednesday	Pumpkin Drink (recipe p.73)	Summer Fruit Salad with Lime & Mint (recipe p.24)	Summer Dinner Salad (recipe p.35)	Stuffed Peppers (recipe p.52)
Thursday	Orange Healthy Smoothie (recipe p.71)	Tropical Granola (recipe p.23)	Salad in Your Hand (recipe p.31)	The Breakup Bowl (recipe p.42)
Friday	Mango, Papaya, Raspberry Smoothie (recipe p.72)	All-American Apple Pie (recipe p.26)	Spicy Sesame Noodle Salad (recipe p.39)	The Fight It Off Bowl (recipe p.43)
Saturday	Basic Green Smoothie (recipe p.74)	Spaghetti Squash Hash Browns (recipe p.30)	Organic Baby Tomato & Kale Salad (recipe p.40)	Angel Hair Pasta with Tomato Sause (recipe p.51)

Hints for Week 1:

- Take it slowly. You do not need to change the world before six o'clock. Give yourself a chance to welcome new ideas and get into a new mood, a new rhythm. Take your time. Calm is good. Speed is stressful.
- Chewing is crucial to getting the most out of your food. It is a fundamental part of the alkaline diet. The quality of your chewing should make up for the smaller quantity of food. The better you chew, the better you will ingest and get all the nutrients from your food. Try to chew each mouthful thirty times.
- Listen to calming, enjoyable music—perhaps something choral or classical. Maybe find a new theme to listen to in the evenings that you enjoy. Discover new composers and genres to go with your diet.
- Buy some colorful flowers and place them around your home where you can appreciate them: in the bathroom, your bedroom, and the kitchen.
- Listen to your body's rhythms and learn to adapt to a better lifestyle. Your body will naturally tell you what it needs, but you have to recognize the good signals and not slip back into bad

habits. For instance, if your body feels tired and you're not at work or doing something important, lie down and have a nap. Be a friend to yourself and your body.

Tips for exercising:

- Regular cardio exercise is an important part of the alkaline diet. Go for a brisk walk. Your pace should be fast enough that you feel your heart beating and your respiratory rate elevating. Try to walk at this pace for half an hour.

<u>Week 2</u>

	Wake up	Breakfast	Lunch	Dinner
Sunday	Liquid Guacamole (recipe p.76)	Breakfast Fajitas (recipe p.28)	Summer Dinner Salad (recipe p.35)	The Hawaiian Bowl (recipe p.44)
Monday	More-Than-a-Mojito Smoothie (recipe p.75)	Brown Rice Porridge (recipe p.29)	Salad in Your Hand (recipe p.31)	BBB Soup (recipe p.57)
Tuesday	Orange, Peach, Kale Smoothie (recipe p.77)	Summer Fruit Salad with Lime & Mint (recipe p.24)	Salad on a Stick (recipe p.33)	The Indian Bowl (recipe p.45)
Wednesday	Orange Healthy Smoothie (recipe p.71)	Spaghetti Squash Hash Browns (recipe p.30)	Organic Baby Tomato & Kale Salad (recipe p.40)	The Rose Bowl (recipe p.48)
Thursday	Tropical Pina Colada Smoothie (recipe p.69)	Baby Potato Home Fries (recipe p.27)	Warm Spinach Salad (recipe p.32)	The Italian Bowl (recipe p.46)
Friday	Pumpkin Drink (recipe p.73)	Good Morning Popeye (recipe p.21)	Spicy Sesame Noodle Salad (recipe p.39)	Thanksgiving Anytime Roasted Vegetables (recipe p.56)
Saturday	Orange Healthy Smoothie (recipe p.71)	Summer Fruit Salad with Lime & Mint (recipe p.24)	Avocado-Caprese Salad (recipe p.38)	The Mexican Bowl (recipe p.47)

Hints for Week 2:

- Turn off the alarm clock and let your body decide how much sleep you really need. Try to wake up naturally at dawn.
- The oils that you have been using throughout the week provide essential omegas in your diet. They are the switches that turn what we eat into nutrition. Blend and vary the oils you use. Flaxseed oil is the most valuable because it is high in omega-3 and makes a great base oil for mixes. But if you don't like the flavor of flaxseed oil, then other nut oils, olive oils, and organic seed oils can be used as they are also immensely important.

- Apply a warm compress to your liver before you go to bed. Wrap a dampened tea towel around a hot water bottle filled with warm water. Lie back and place it underneath your ribs and to the right. Leave for fifteen minutes or even all night.
- Switch off the television and your computer, and put your cell phone aside. Try to enjoy a relaxing evening without the buzz of the outside world.

Tips for exercising:

- Go for a jog or, if you have the equipment, use an elliptical for at least half an hour. Try to fluctuate your pace while jogging: every five minutes, increase your pace by thirty percent for a minute.
- Go for a bike ride either on a bike outside or a stationary bike. Aim for half an hour and try to challenge yourself with different inclines and gears. Cycling will tone and strengthen your legs, thighs, and glutes. It is a lower impact activity than running, and it can also relieve back pain and muscle strain on your feet and knees.

<u>Week 3</u>

	Wake up	Breakfast	Lunch	Dinner
Sunday	More-Than-a-Mojito Smoothie (recipe p.75)	Good Morning Popeye (recipe p.21)	Salad in Your Hand (recipe p.31)	Date Night Garlic Bake (recipe p.55)
Monday	Liquid Guacamole (recipe p.76)	Baby Potato Home Fries (recipe p.27)	Salad on a Stick (recipe p.33)	Curried Eggplant (recipe p.53)
Tuesday	Orange Healthy Smoothie (recipe p.71)	Garden Pancakes (recipe p.22)	Summer Dinner Salad (recipe p.35)	Championship Chili (recipe p.54)
Wednesday	Tropical Pina Colada Smoothie (recipe p.69)	Summer Fruit Salad with Lime & Mint (recipe p.24)	Warm Spinach Salad (recipe p.32)	Better than Chicken Soup (recipe p.50)
Thursday	Pumpkin Drink (recipe p.73)	All-American Apple Pie (recipe p.26)	Emeraland Forest Salad (recipe p.34)	The Southern Bowl (recipe p.49)
Friday	Tropical Pina Colada Smoothie (recipe p.69)	Tropical Granola (recipe p.23)	Roasted Vegetable Salad (recipe p.36)	Stuffed Peppers (recipe p.52)
Saturday	Orange, Peach, Kale Smoothie (recipe p.77)	Spaghetti Squash Hash Browns (recipe p.30)	Quinoa & Avocado Salad (recipe p.37)	Angel Hair Pasta with Tomato Sause (recipe p.51)

Hints for Week 3:

- Most of us eat too much. Cut your portion sizes down. At restaurants, do not be tempted to eat everything on your plate. At home, use small plates rather than big ones. Mix up your mealt to

keep things interesting. Eat slower so that you take the same amount of time for dinner but eat less. Put your cutlery down between mouthfuls.
- Buy some houseplants. They will improve the oxygen circulation in your rooms and lend a calming presence to your décor.
- Keep up your routines—exercising, preparing meals, dry skin rushing, bathing, sleeping. Routine is an immensely strong thing. The body prepares itself better if things are regular. Hormones have a twenty-four-hour cycle and are easily disturbed. In order to reset their balance, you need to have a regular routine.
- You have cleaned your system, now clean out your home. Get rid of useless things and establish an orderly living environment.

Tips for exercising:

- As a reward for your efforts these weeks, take a gentle stroll this evening and enjoy your alkaline body.
- Get a reflexology massage. The massage focuses on reflex areas on your feet that are connected to parts of your body in order to relax these areas and open the energy flow. It promotes circulation and general healing.

CHAPTER 3. Recipes
BREAKFAST

Good Morning Popeye

Prep time: 5 minutes

Cooking time: 10 minutes

Servings: 2

Nutrients per serving:

Carbohydrates – 37.8 g

Fiber – 8.1 g

Fat – 1.5 g

Protein – 5.6 g

Calories – 181

Ingredients:

- 1 Tbsp coconut oil
- 2 medium sweet potatoes, peeled and cubed
- 1 medium sweet onion, chopped
- 1 red bell pepper, seeded, chopped
- ¼ cup sliced mushrooms, any type
- 2 garlic cloves, chopped
- 4 cups spinach
- 1 tsp onion powder
- 1 tsp garlic powder
- ½ tsp Bouquet Garni herb blend, or other dried herbs such as rosemary or sage
- ½ tsp sea salt

Instructions:

1. In a medium bowl, combine the oil, sweet potatoes, onion, red bell pepper, mushrooms, garlic, spinach, onion powder, garlic powder, Bouquet Garni, and salt.
2. Toss the vegetables in the oil until evenly coated.
3. Heat a nonstick frying pan over medium heat and cook the vegetables, stirring, for 10 minutes, or until tender.
4. Divide into two portions and serve.

Garden Pancakes

Prep time: 5 minutes

Cooking time: 5 minutes

Servings: 2

Nutrients per serving:

Carbohydrates – 33.4 g

Fiber – 7.2 g

Fat – 12.1 g

Protein – 6.3 g

Calories – 254

Ingredients:

- 1 medium zucchini, roughly chopped
- 1 carrot, peeled and roughly chopped
- 1 yellow squash, roughly chopped
- ½ small white onion, grated
- 4 scallions
- ¼ cup almond flour
- 1 tsp sea salt
- ½ tsp garlic powder
- ¼ cup filtered water, as needed

Instructions:

1. Place the zucchini, carrot, yellow squash, onion, scallions, almond flour, salt, and garlic powder in a food processor. Pulse until blended.
2. Add water to make the mixture moist, not runny. The batter will be fairly thick.
3. Spray a nonstick skillet or griddle with cooking spray and heat over medium-high heat.
4. Use an ice cream scoop or ¼-cup measure to drop the batter into the skillet. With a fork, spread the batter evenly, pressing down on the pancakes. Cook, turning once, until browned on both sides, 5 minutes total.
5. Serve hot or at room temperature.

Tropical Granola

Prep time: 2 minutes

Cooking time: 15 minutes

Servings: 4

Nutrients per serving:

Carbohydrates – 44 g

Fiber – 3.8 g

Fat – 0.3 g

Protein – 2.3 g

Calories – 182

Ingredients:

- 1 cup flaked unsweetened coconut
- 1 cup slivered almonds
- ½ cup flaxseed
- ½ cup raisins
- ½ tsp cinnamon
- ¼ tsp ginger
- ¼ tsp nutmeg
- ¼ tsp sea salt
- 1 vanilla bean, split lengthwise, deseeded
- ¼ cup coconut oil
- ½ cup unsweetened dried pineapple tidbits

Instructions:

1. Preheat oven to 350° F.
2. In a medium bowl, combine the coconut, almonds, flaxseed, raisins, cinnamon, ginger, nutmeg, salt, vanilla bean seeds, and coconut oil. Mix until well combined.

3. Spread the mixture on a baking sheet and bake for 15 minutes, occasionally stirring, until golden brown.
4. Remove from the oven and cool, without stirring.
5. Once cooled, stir in the pineapple tidbits.
6. Store in an airtight container.

Summer Fruit Salad with Lime & Mint

Prep time: 10 minutes

Cooking time: 0 minutes

Servings: 4

Nutrients per serving:

Carbohydrates – 7.8 g

Fiber – 0.09 g

Fat – 0.02 g

Protein – 0.6 g

Calories – 32

Ingredients:

- ¼ cup grapes
- ¼ cup peeled and diced apple
- ¼ cup bite-size watermelon pieces
- ¼ cup bite-size honeydew melon pieces
- ¼ cup bite-size cantaloupe pieces
- ¼ cup tangerine slices
- ¼ cup peeled and diced peaches
- ¼ cup strawberries
- 2 Tbsp chopped fresh mint
- 2 Tbsp freshly squeezed lemon juice

Instructions:

1. In a medium bowl, combine all fruit.
2. Add the mint and lemon juice and mix well. Cover and refrigerate overnight.
3. Serve chilled.

Winter Fruit Compote with Figs & Ginger

Prep time: 10 minutes

Cooking time: 10 minutes

Servings: 4

Nutrients per serving:

Carbohydrates – 26 g

Fiber – 4.2 g

Fat – 0.4 g

Protein – 1 g

Calories – 102

Ingredients:

- 2 small tangerines, peeled, sectioned
- 1 apple, peeled, cored, diced
- ½ cup figs, stemmed and quartered
- ½ cup dried plums, halved
- ¼ cup dark cherries
- 1 cup filtered water
- 1 vanilla bean, split lengthwise, deseeded
- 1 tsp fresh ginger, grated
- ½ tsp cinnamon
- ½ tsp cloves
- 1 packet stevia (optional)

Instructions:

1. In a medium saucepan, combine all ingredients.
2. Bring to a simmer over medium heat and cook, occasionally stirring, for 10 minutes, or until the fruit is tender but not too soft.
3. Remove from heat and let stand for 30 minutes.
4. Reheat if necessary, and serve warm.

All-American Apple Pie

Prep time: 10 minutes

Cooking time: 10 minutes

Servings: 4

Nutrients per serving:

Carbohydrates – 28.5 g

Fiber – 4.5 g

Fat – 0.1 g

Protein – 0.2 g

Calories – 109

Ingredients:

- 4 apples, peeled, cored, sliced
- ½ cup orange juice, freshly squeezed
- 1 vanilla bean, cut lengthwise, deseeded
- ¼ tsp cinnamon
- ¼ cup unsweetened coconut milk

Instructions:

1. In a bowl, combine all ingredients.
2. In a skillet set over medium heat, add the fruit mixture. Cook for 10 minutes.
3. Divide the mixture among four serving dishes and serve warm.
4. Top with 1 Tbsp coconut milk.

Baby Potato Home Fries

Prep time: 5 minutes

Cooking time: 20 minutes

Servings: 2

Nutrients per serving:

Carbohydrates – 74.8 g

Fiber – 12.4 g

Fat – 0.8 g

Protein – 9.3 g

Calories – 337

Ingredients:

- 4 medium baby white potatoes
- ¼ cup vegetable broth
- ½ sweet white onion, chopped
- 1 red bell pepper, seeded, diced
- ½ cup mushrooms, sliced, any type
- 1 tsp sea salt
- 1 tsp garlic powder

Instructions:

1. In a medium microwave-safe bowl, microwave the potatoes for 4 minutes, or until soft. Let cool.
2. In a large nonstick skillet set over medium heat, add the broth, onion, and red bell pepper. Sauté the vegetables for 5 minutes.
3. While the onion and peppers cook, cut the potatoes into quarters.
4. Add the potatoes, mushrooms, salt, and garlic powder to the skillet. Stir to combine. Cook for 10 minutes until the potatoes are crisp.
5. Serve warm.

Breakfast Fajitas

Prep time: 5 minutes

Cooking time: 10 minutes

Servings: 2

Nutrients per serving:

Carbohydrates – 17.4 g

Fiber – 5.1 g

Fat – 0.07 g

Protein – 4.1 g

Calories – 86

Ingredients:

- 1 bell pepper, any color, seeded, sliced
- 1 sweet onion, chopped
- 1 cup cooked broccoli florets
- ½ cup mushrooms, sliced
- 1 cup cherry tomatoes, halved if large
- ½ cup sliced zucchini, or other squash
- 2 garlic cloves, peeled, chopped
- 1 jalapeño, chopped
- 1 tsp sea salt
- ½ tsp cumin
- 2 Tbsp fresh cilantro
- Juice of ½ lime

Instructions:

1. Spray a nonstick skillet with cooking spray and place it over medium heat.
2. Add the bell pepper, onion, broccoli, mushrooms, tomatoes, zucchini, garlic, and jalapeño. Cook for 7 minutes, or until the desired level of tenderness, occasionally stirring.
3. Stir in the salt, cumin, and cilantro. Cook, stirring, for 3 minutes more.
4. Remove from heat and add the lime juice.
5. Divide between two plates and serve.

Brown Rice Porridge

Prep time: 5 minutes

Cooking time: 5 minutes

Servings: 6

Nutrients per serving:

Carbohydrates – 48.3 g

Fiber – 3.6 g

Fat – 1.8 g

Protein – 7 g

Calories – 236

Ingredients:

- 3 cups cooked brown rice
- 1 cup almond milk
- 1 packet stevia

Instructions:

1. In a saucepan, combine the brown rice and the almond milk. Simmer over medium heat for 5 minutes, constantly stirring, until the mixture is thick and creamy.
2. Remove from heat and stir in the stevia.
3. Divide among 6 bowls and serve.

Spaghetti Squash Hash Browns

Prep time: 2 minutes

Cooking time: 10 minutes

Servings: 2

Nutrients per serving:

Carbohydrates – 9.7 g

Fiber – 0.6 g

Fat – 0.6 g

Protein – 0.9 g

Calories – 44

Ingredients:

- 2 cups cooked spaghetti squash
- ½ cup onion, finely chopped
- 1 tsp garlic powder
- ½ tsp sea salt

Instructions:

1. Using paper towel, squeeze any excess moisture from the spaghetti squash. Place the squash in a medium bowl. Add the onion, garlic powder, and salt. Mix to combine.
2. Spray a nonstick skillet with cooking spray and place it over medium heat.
3. Add the squash mixture to the pan. Cook, untouched, for 5 minutes. With a spatula, flip the hash browns. It's okay if the mixture falls apart. Cook for 5 minutes more until the desired level of crispness.

SALADS

Salad in Your Hand

Prep time: 10 minutes

Cooking time: 0 minutes

Servings: 1

Nutrients per serving:

Carbohydrates – 17.8 g

Fiber – 6.5 g

Fat – 13.1 g

Protein – 4.1 g

Calories – 189

Ingredients:

- 4 leaves lettuce, iceberg or romaine
- ½ avocado, diced
- 1 carrot, peeled, shredded
- ½ tomato, diced
- 1/3 cucumber, peeled, diced
- 1 Tbsp almonds, chopped

Instructions:

1. Mix the avocado, carrot, cucumber, tomato, and almonds together.
2. Fill each leaf with one-quarter each of the mix and roll up.

Warm Spinach Salad

Prep time: 2 minutes

Cooking time: 5 minutes

Servings: 2

Nutrients per serving:

Carbohydrates – 20.3 g

Fiber – 7.6 g

Fat – 19.4 g

Protein – 10.2 g

Calories – 271

Ingredients:

- 1 6-oz package baby spinach leaves
- ½ cup almonds, chopped, toasted
- 1 Tbsp sesame oil
- 1 Tbsp apple cider vinegar
- 1 tsp sea salt
- 1 cup shiitake mushrooms, chopped
- Water, as needed

Instructions:

1. In a bowl, combine the spinach and almonds.
2. In a small saucepan over low heat, combine the sesame oil, cider vinegar, salt, and mushrooms. Cook for 5 minutes, adding water if it is absorbed.
3. Drizzle the mushroom dressing over the spinach and toss well to coat the spinach leaves.
4. Serve immediately.

Salad on a Stick

Prep time: 5 minutes

Cooking time: 0 minutes

Servings: 2

Nutrients per serving:

Carbohydrates – 31.2 g

Fiber – 8.9 g

Fat – 1.5 g

Protein – 7.8 g

Calories – 142

Ingredients:

- 1 zucchini, sliced into 8 pieces
- 1 yellow squash, sliced into 8 pieces
- 1 cucumber, sliced into 8 pieces
- 8 cherry tomatoes
- 8 steamed broccoli florets
- 8 cauliflower florets
- 2 Tbsp blue cheese dressing

Instructions:

1. On a wooden skewer, thread 1 zucchini slice, 1 yellow squash slice, 1 cucumber slice, 1 cherry tomato, 1 broccoli floret, and 1 cauliflower floret.
2. Repeat the process with remaining skewers and ingredients.
3. Drizzle with blue cheese dressing.

Emeraland Forest Salad

Prep time: 5 minutes

Cooking time: 0 minutes

Servings: 4

Nutrients per serving:

Carbohydrates – 53 g

Fiber – 6.2 g

Fat – 11.8 g

Protein – 12.2 g

Calories – 364

Ingredients:

- 1 cup cooked broccoli florets, roughly chopped
- 1 cup asparagus spears, trimmed, cooked roughly chopped
- 2 cups cooked quinoa, cooled
- ½ cup water
- 2 Tbsp lemon juice, freshly squeezed
- 2 Tbsp coconut oil
- ½ tsp sea salt

Instructions:

1. In a bowl, combine the broccoli and asparagus.
2. Stir in the quinoa.
3. In a blender, combine the water, lemon juice, coconut oil, and salt. Blend until the ingredients emulsify. Pour the dressing over the salad. Stir to combine.
4. Refrigerate the salad for 15 minutes to chill.
5. Serve cold.

Summer Dinner Salad

Prep time: 5 minutes

Cooking time: 0 minutes

Servings: 4

Nutrients per serving:

Carbohydrates – 9 g

Fiber – 2.1 g

Fat – 0.3 g

Protein – 1.6 g

Calories – 39

Ingredients:

- 4 cups chopped iceberg or romaine lettuce
- 2 cups cherry tomatoes, halved
- 1 14.5-oz can whole green beans, drained
- 1/2 cup carrot, shredded
- 1 scallion, sliced
- 1 cucumber, peeled, sliced
- 2 radishes, thinly sliced

Instructions:

1. In a bowl, combine all ingredients and toss with 2 Tbsp of your favorite dressing.

Roasted Vegetable Salad

Prep time: 10 minutes

Cooking time: 15 minutes

Servings: 2

Nutrients per serving:

Carbohydrates – 15.4 g

Fiber – 4.2 g

Fat – 7.3 g

Protein – 2.9 g

Calories – 132

Ingredients:

- 2 cups asparagus, chopped
- 1 pint cherry tomatoes
- ½ cup mushrooms halved
- 1 carrot, peeled, cut into bite-size pieces
- 1 red bell pepper, seeded, roughly chopped
- 1 Tbsp coconut oil
- 1 Tbsp garlic powder
- 1 tsp sea salt

Instructions:

1. Preheat the oven to 425°F.
2. In a bowl, combine all ingredients, coating the vegetables evenly.
3. Transfer the vegetables to a baking pan and roast for 15 minutes, or until the vegetables are tender.
4. Transfer the vegetables to a large bowl and serve either warm or cold.

Quinoa & Avocado Salad

Prep time: 10 minutes

Cooking time: 0 minutes

Servings: 2

Nutrients per serving:

Carbohydrates – 63.6 g

Fiber – 9.9 g

Fat – 14.8 g

Protein – 13.7 g

Calories – 433

Ingredients:

- 1 cup cooked quinoa, cooled
- 1 avocado, cut into cubes
- 5 oz fresh spinach, roughly chopped
- 1 cup cherry tomatoes, halved
- 1 cup cucumber, peeled, diced
- ¼ cup chopped cilantro
- 1 Tbsp garlic powder
- 1 Tbsp onion powder
- 1 tsp sea salt
- 1 Tbsp lemon juice, freshly squeezed

Instructions:

1. In a bowl, combine all ingredients.
2. Chill for 15 minutes to allow the flavors to blend.
3. Serve immediately, or keep refrigerated for 2 to 3 days.

Avocado-Caprese Salad

Prep time: 5 minutes

Cooking time: 0 minutes

Servings: 2

Nutrients per serving:

Carbohydrates – 9.1 g

Fiber – 4.9 g

Fat – 10.1 g

Protein – 2 g

Calories – 125

Ingredients:

- 2 large heirloom tomatoes, sliced
- 1 avocado, sliced
- 1 bunch basil leaves
- 1 tsp sea salt

Instructions:

1. In a bowl, toss all ingredients.
2. Season with the salt and serve.

Spicy Sesame Noodle Salad

Prep time: 10 minutes

Cooking time: 0 minutes

Servings: 4

Nutrients per serving:

Carbohydrates – 6.4 g

Fiber – 2.5 g

Fat – 6 g

Protein – 2.5 g

Calories – 111

Ingredients:

- 1 roasted spaghetti squash
- 2 cups cooked broccoli florets
- 1 bell pepper, seeded, cut into strips
- 1 scallion, chopped
- 1 Tbsp sesame oil
- 1 tsp red pepper flakes
- 1 tsp sea salt
- 2 Tbsp toasted sesame seeds

Instructions:

1. Prepare the spaghetti squash "noodles" by removing the inside of the cooked squash with a fork into a large bowl.
2. Add the broccoli, red bell pepper, and scallion.
3. In a separate bowl, combine the sesame oil, red pepper flakes, and salt. Drizzle atop the vegetables. Toss gently to combine.
4. Garnish with the sesame seeds and serve.

Organic Baby Tomato & Kale Salad

Prep time: 10 minutes

Cooking time: 0 minutes

Servings: 2

Nutrients per serving:

Carbohydrates – 1.6 g

Fiber – 6.8 g

Fat – 6.9 g

Protein – 1.1 g

Calories – 58

Ingredients:

- 1 bunch kale, stemmed, leaves washed, chopped
- 2 cups organic baby tomatoes
- 2 Tbsp Ranch Dressing

Instructions:

1. In a bowl, combine all ingredients.
2. Divide equally onto two serving plates and enjoy immediately.

BOWLS

The Asian Bowl

Prep time: 5 minutes

Cooking time: 0 minutes

Servings: 1

Nutrients per serving:

Carbohydrates – 20.8 g

Fiber – 6.6 g

Fat – 24.7 g

Protein – 7.2 g

Calories – 317

Ingredients:

- 1 cup green cabbage, shredded
- 1 cup red cabbage, shredded
- 1 cup carrots, chopped
- ¼ cup water chestnuts
- 3 Tbsp scallions, chopped
- 1 Tbsp dark sesame oil
- 1 Tbsp cashew butter
- ¼ tsp red pepper flakes, or additional as needed
- ½ tsp ginger powder
- Hot water, as needed
- 2 tsp toasted sesame seeds

Instructions:

1. In a medium bowl, layer the green and red cabbage, then the carrots, water chestnuts, and scallions.
2. In a blender, add the sesame oil, cashew butter, red pepper flakes, and ginger powder. Blend until the ingredients emulsify. Add hot water by the teaspoon, if the dressing is too thick.
3. Pour the dressing over the vegetables, add sesame seeds, and serve.

The Breakup Bowl

Prep time: 5 minutes

Cooking time: 0 minutes

Servings: 1

Nutrients per serving:

Carbohydrates – 69.4 g

Fiber – 9.6 g

Fat – 19.2 g

Protein – 6.9 g

Calories – 454

Ingredients:

- 2 frozen bananas
- 2 Tbsp coconut milk
- 2 Tbsp fruit-sweetened-only strawberry jam
- 2 Tbsp unsweetened coconut, grated
- 2 Tbsp almonds, chopped, toasted
- ¼ cup coconut whipped cream

Instructions:

1. In a food processor, combine bananas and coconut milk, blending until the mixture takes on the consistency of ice cream. Transfer to a single-serving bowl.
2. Top with the jam, coconut, toasted almonds, and whipped cream.
3. Serve immediately.

The Fight It Off Bowl

Prep time: 5 minutes

Cooking time: 10 minutes

Servings: 1

Nutrients per serving:

Carbohydrates – 12.8 g

Fiber – 2.8 g

Fat – 2.9 g

Protein – 11.8 g

Calories – 126

Ingredients:

- 2 cups vegetable broth
- 1 carrot, peeled, sliced
- ½ cup bite-size broccoli florets
- 2 garlic cloves, finely minced

Instructions:

1. In a saucepan over medium heat, combine all ingredients. Cook for 10 minutes, or until vegetables reach a desired level of tenderness.
2. Pour into a bowl and eat.

The Hawaiian Bowl

Prep time: 5 minutes

Cooking time: 5 minutes

Servings: 1

Nutrients per serving:

Carbohydrates – 47.6 g

Fiber – 4.6 g

Fat – 1.6 g

Protein – 3.6 g

Calories – 223

Ingredients:

- ½ cup cooked brown rice
- 1 cup steamed broccoli
- ¼ cup packed-in-juice pineapple chunks, drained, liquid reserved
- 2 tbsp barbecue sauce

Instructions:

1. In a medium bowl, layer the brown rice, broccoli, and pineapple.
2. In a saucepan over medium heat, whisk together the reserved pineapple juice and the barbecue sauce for 5 minutes, until thickened and bubbly.
3. Pour over the rice and broccoli and serve.

The Indian Bowl

Prep time: 10 minutes

Cooking time: 5 minutes

Servings: 1

Nutrients per serving:

Carbohydrates – 26.1 g

Fiber – 13.5 g

Fat – 0.2 g

Protein – 5.4 g

Calories – 469

Ingredients:

- 1 cup cooked quinoa, warmed
- 1 large carrot, peeled, sliced, steamed
- ½ cup cauliflower florets, cooked
- ⅛ cup chickpeas
- ¼ cup mushrooms, sliced
- ½ cup coconut milk
- 1 Tbsp yellow curry powder
- ½ tsp ground ginger
- 1 tsp sea salt
- 1 Tbsp tomato paste

Instructions:

1. In a medium bowl, layer the quinoa, carrot, cauliflower, and chickpeas.
2. In a saucepan over medium heat, combine the mushrooms, coconut milk, curry powder, ginger, salt, and tomato paste. Whisk until the mixture simmers. Cook for 5 minutes and then let cool slightly.
3. Pour the sauce over the quinoa mixture and serve immediately.

The Italian Bowl

Prep time: 5 minutes

Cooking time: 10 minutes

Servings: 1

Nutrients per serving:

Carbohydrates – 71.5 g

Fiber – 10.8 g

Fat – 5.4 g

Protein – 14.5 g

Calories – 390

Ingredients:

- 1 14.5-oz can tomatoes, whole, diced, or crushed, undrained
- 1 medium onion, diced
- ½ cup zucchini, sliced
- 4 garlic cloves, minced
- 1/3 cup fresh basil, chopped
- ½ tsp fresh oregano, chopped
- 2 Tbsp lemon juice, freshly squeezed
- 1 cup cooked quinoa, warmed
- ½ cup eggplant, peeled, diced, cooked, rewarmed

Instructions:

1. Drain 2 tablespoons of liquid from the tomatoes and add it to a medium saucepan set over medium heat. Sir in the onion and sauté for 5 minutes, or until translucent.
2. Add the tomatoes with their remaining juices, zucchini, garlic, basil, and oregano. Stir to combine. Simmer for 5 minutes. Add the lemon juice.
3. In a single-serving bowl, layer the quinoa and the eggplant. Top with the tomato mixture.
4. Serve warm.

The Mexican Bowl

Prep time: 10 minutes

Cooking time: 0 minutes

Servings: 1

Nutrients per serving:

Carbohydrates – 69.5 g

Fiber – 17.4 g

Fat – 11.4 g

Protein – 17.8 g

Calories – 436

Ingredients:

- 1 cup sprouted black beans
- 1 tsp cumin, ground
- 1 medium sweet potato, cooked, diced
- 2/3 cup corn kernels
- ½ cup cilantro, chopped
- ½ avocado, diced
- 3 Tbsp salsa fresca
- Pinch sea salt

Instructions:

1. In a small bowl, combine the beans, corn and the cumin.
2. In a medium microwaveable bowl, layer the sweet potatoes and top with the beans. Warm the vegetables in the microwave on high for 2 minutes, or until heated through.
3. Remove from the microwave and layer on the cilantro and avocado, and top with the salsa.
4. Season with salt and serve immediately.

The Rose Bowl

Prep time: 5 minutes

Cooking time: 2 minutes

Servings: 1

Nutrients per serving:

Carbohydrates – 64.5 g

Fiber – 6.7 g

Fat – 1.8 g

Protein – 16.7 g

Calories – 401

Ingredients:

- 1 cup red quinoa, cooked
- ½ cup red peppers, roasted, diced
- ½ cup dark red cherries, pitted, sliced
- ¾ tsp red curry paste
- ½ cup coconut milk

Instructions:

1. In a single-serving bowl, layer the quinoa, red peppers, and cherries.
2. In a blender, mix together the curry paste and coconut milk. Pour the liquid over the layered quinoa, peppers, and cherries.
3. Microwave on high for 2 minutes.

The Southern Bowl

Prep time: 5 minutes

Cooking time: 50 minutes

Servings: 1

Nutrients per serving:

Carbohydrates – 37.5 g

Fiber – 7.3 g

Fat – 2.7 g

Protein – 9 g

Calories – 201

Ingredients:

- ¼ cup vegetable broth, divided
- ¼ sweet onion, chopped
- 1 garlic clove, finely chopped
- ½ tsp sea salt, divided
- 4 ounces canned tomatoes, diced
- 1 cup collard greens
- 1 okra, fresh or frozen, sliced
- 1 sweet potato, peeled, cut into bite-size pieces
- ¼ cup almond milk

Instructions:

1. In a saucepan over medium heat, heat 2 Tbsp vegetable broth. Add the onion and sauté for 5 minutes, or until translucent.
2. Add the garlic, ¼ tsp salt, tomatoes, the remaining 2 Tbsp broth, collard greens, and okra. Simmer for 30-35 minutes, or until tender.
3. In a pot of boiling water, cook the sweet potato pieces for 10 minutes, or until tender. Drain and place in a medium bowl.
4. To the potatoes, add the almond milk and remaining ¼ tsp salt. Using an electric mixer, mash the sweet potatoes.
5. Place the warm mashed sweet potato in a bowl. In another bowl, add the collard greens and okra mixture.

MAIN DISHES

Better than Chicken Soup

Prep time: 15 minutes

Cooking time: 1 hour 10 minutes

Servings: 4

Nutrients per serving:

Carbohydrates – 37.8 g

Fiber – 8.1 g

Fat – 1.5 g

Protein – 5.6 g

Calories – 181

Ingredients:

- 1 onion, roughly chopped
- 2 carrots, peeled, roughly chopped
- 2 celery stalks , roughly chopped
- 1 parsnip, peeled, roughly chopped
- 5 garlic cloves, smashed
- 1 leek, cleaned well, roughly chopped
- 9 cups water
- 2 bay leaves
- 2 tsp sea salt

Instructions:

1. Spray the bottom of a stockpot with cooking spray. Place the pot over medium-low heat and sauté onion for about 5 minutes, stirring constantly.
2. Add the carrots, celery, parsnip, garlic, and leek to the pot. Sauté for another 3 minutes.
3. Add the water, bay leaves, and salt. Simmer for 1 hour.
4. Remove from the heat and cool slightly. Strain out the vegetables, leaving only the broth.
5. To serve, add back some of the vegetables if you wish and warm the soup to the desired temperature.

Angel Hair Pasta with Tomato Sause

Prep time: 15 minutes

Cooking time: 15 minutes

Servings: 2

Nutrients per serving:

Carbohydrates – 36.8 g

Fiber – 7.7 g

Fat – 3.8 g

Protein – 8.6 g

Calories – 284

Ingredients:

- ¼ onion, chopped
- 1 tsp coconut oil
- 1 tsp sea salt
- 1 tsp minced garlic
- ½ tsp red pepper flakes
- 1 6-oz can tomato paste
- 1 16-oz jar spaghetti sauce
- ½ cup water
- 2 cups cooked spaghetti squash, shredded

Instructions:

1. In a medium pot set over medium heat, sauté the onion in the coconut oil for about 5 minutes, or until tender.
2. Add the salt, garlic, red pepper flakes, and tomato paste. Stir well.
3. Add the spaghetti sauce and water. Simmer for 10 minutes.
4. Stir in the spaghetti squash and combine.
5. Serve immediately.

Stuffed Peppers

Prep time: 5 minutes

Cooking time: 20 minutes

Servings: 2

Nutrients per serving:

Carbohydrates – 34.8 g

Fiber – 7.2 g

Fat – 5.1 g

Protein – 7.2 g

Calories – 213

Ingredients:

- 1 tsp coconut oil
- ½ cup chopped vegetables, zucchini, carrots, or broccoli
- 1 cup quinoa, cooked
- 1 tsp garlic powder
- 1 tsp onion powder
- 1 tsp sea salt
- 2 bell peppers, any color, cored, seeded; tops removed, reserved

Instructions:

1. Preheat oven to 350°F.
2. Coat a baking pan with cooking spray.
3. In a saucepan over medium heat, sauté the vegetables (except for the bell peppers) in coconut oil for 5 minutes, or until softened.
4. Add the quinoa, garlic powder, onion powder, and salt. Stir to combine.
5. Place each bell pepper upright in the prepared pan. Fill each pepper with one-half of the quinoa-vegetable mix. Top each pepper with its reserved top.
6. Cover with aluminum foil and bake for 15 minutes, or until the peppers are soft.

Curried Eggplant

Prep time: 5 minutes

Cooking time: 5 minutes

Servings: 2

Nutrients per serving:

Carbohydrates – 14.1 g

Fiber – 8.4 g

Fat – 2.8 g

Protein – 2.4 g

Calories – 81

Ingredients:

- Flesh of 1 roasted eggplant
- Juice of 1 lemon
- 1 tsp sea salt
- 1 tsp sesame oil
- 1 tsp curry powder
- Water, as needed
- Cooked quinoa, for serving

Instructions:

1. In a food processor, combine the eggplant, lemon juice, salt, sesame oil, and curry powder. Blend until smooth.
2. To a saucepan set over medium heat, transfer the eggplant mixture and warm it for about 5 minutes. Add some water to thin, if necessary.
3. Serve as is, or over quinoa.

Championship Chili

Prep time: 5 minutes

Cooking time: 25 minutes

Servings: 4

Nutrients per serving:

Carbohydrates – 18.5 g

Fiber – 5.3 g

Fat – 2.7 g

Protein – 3.9 g

Calories – 101

Ingredients:

- 1 small onion, chopped
- 1 cup red bell pepper, diced
- 2 garlic cloves, finely chopped
- 2 cups sprouted beans, black, kidney, or pinto
- 1 14.5-oz canned tomatoes, diced
- 2 Tbsp barbecue sauce
- 1 8-oz jar organic pasta sauce
- 1/4 cup organic salsa, mild, medium, or hot
- 1/4 cup organic fresh cilantro
- Dash chili powder
- Dash ground cumin

Instructions:

1. Spray a medium-size pot with cooking spray. Over medium heat, sauté the onion for 5 minutes, or until soft and slightly caramelized.
2. Add remaining ingredients and stir to combine. Simmer for 20 minutes.
3. Serve immediately.

Date Night Broccoli Bake

Prep time: 10 minutes

Cooking time: 30 minutes

Servings: 2

Nutrients per serving:

Carbohydrates – 28.1 g

Fiber – 5.1 g

Fat – 15.2 g

Protein – 11.6 g

Calories – 270

Ingredients:

- 1 lb broccoli, cut into bite-size pieces
- 4 carrots, peeled, sliced lengthwise
- 3 garlic heads, cloves peeled, chopped,
- 2 tsp lemon zest
- 1 tsp sea salt
- ¼ tsp mustard powder
- 1 cup vegetable broth
- 2 Tbsp coconut oil

Instructions:

1. Preheat the oven to 400°F.
2. In a bowl, combine all ingredients.
3. Evenly spread the mixture into a baking pan. Cover with aluminum foil and place in the preheated oven. Bake for 30 minutes, stirring once.
4. Serve immediately.

Thanksgiving Anytime Roasted Vegetables

Prep time: 15 minutes

Cooking time: 1 hour

Servings: 4

Nutrients per serving:

Carbohydrates – 44.3 g

Fiber – 6.3 g

Fat – 12.4 g

Protein – 4.1 g

Calories – 176

Ingredients:

- 1 butternut squash, peeled, cubed
- 1 baking pumpkin, peeled, cubed
- 2 large carrots, peeled, cubed
- 2 green apples, peeled, cored, chopped
- 3 fresh sage leaves, finely chopped
- 1 tsp sea salt
- 2 tsp coconut oil

Instructions:

1. Preheat oven to 350°F.
2. In a bowl, toss all ingredients together until evenly coated in the oil and seasonings. Transfer the vegetables to a roasting pan in a single layer.
3. Roast for 60 minutes, stirring occasionally. Serve.

BBB Soup

Prep time: 5 minutes

Cooking time: 10 minutes

Servings: 2

Nutrients per serving:

Carbohydrates – 38.5 g

Fiber – 2.7 g

Fat – 3.5 g

Protein – 11.7 g

Calories – 172

Ingredients:

- 3 cups vegetable broth
- 1 cup bok choy, chopped
- 1 bunch broccolini, chopped roughly
- ½ cup brown rice, cooked
- 2-3 carrots, peeled, sliced

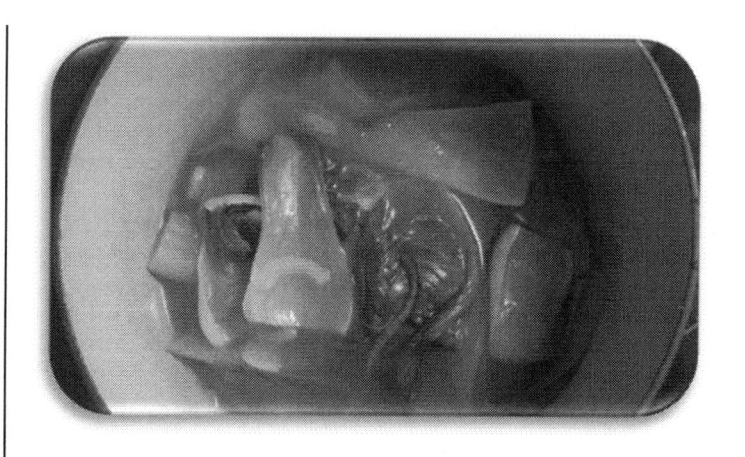

Instructions:

1. In a saucepan over medium heat, combine all ingredients.
2. Bring to a simmer and cook for 10 minutes, or until the vegetables are cooked and tender. Serve.

Grilled Vegetables Stack

Prep time: 10 minutes

Cooking time: 20 minutes

Servings: 2

Nutrients per serving:

Carbohydrates – 15.7 g

Fiber – 3.6 g

Fat – 3.1 g

Protein – 3.9 g

Calories – 179

Ingredients:

- 2 portobello mushrooms, stemmed, gills removed
- ½ eggplant, sliced into ¼-inch-thick slices
- 1 yellow bell pepper, seeded, sliced lengthwise
- 1 red bell pepper, seeded, sliced lengthwise
- 1 red onion, peeled, sliced
- ½ cup hummus, divided
- 1 tsp sea salt, divided

Instructions:

1. Preheat the grill or a broiler.
2. Over medium coals or a gas flame, grill the mushroom caps, eggplant, yellow bell peppers, red bell peppers, and onion for 20 minutes, turning occasionally.
3. Fill one mushroom cap with ¼ cup of hummus. Top with half of the eggplant, yellow peppers, red peppers, and onion slices. Sprinkle ½ tsp of salt on top. Set aside.
4. Repeat with the second mushroom cap and remaining ingredients. Serve warm.

No BS Brussels Sprouts

Prep time: 5 minutes

Cooking time: 10 minutes

Servings: 2

Nutrients per serving:

Carbohydrates – 19.4 g

Fiber – 6.5 g

Fat – 8.7 g

Protein – 7.9 g

Calories – 169

Ingredients:

- ½ cup light unsweetened coconut milk
- 1 tsp lime juice, freshly squeezed
- 1½ tsp ground ginger
- ½ tsp chili-garlic sauce
- 1 packet stevia
- ¾ pound Brussels sprouts, ends removed, trimmed, halved
- 1 Tbsp coconut oil
- ½ tsp sea salt

Instructions:

1. In a saucepan over medium heat, combine the coconut milk, lime juice, ground ginger, chili-garlic sauce, and stevia. Bring ingredients to a simmer. Cook for 5 minutes. Remove from heat and set aside.
2. In a bowl, add the Brussels sprouts, coconut oil, and sea salt. Toss to combine.
3. Transfer to a medium cast-iron pan or ovenproof skillet. Sauté over medium heat for 5 minutes.
4. Preheat the broiler. Broil for 3 minutes, or until the leaves are slightly browned.
5. Transfer the Brussels sprouts to a bowl. Add the sauce and toss to coat.
6. Serve immediately.

Sprouted Beans

Prep time: 3-4 days

Cooking time: 0 minutes

Servings: 4

Nutrients per serving:

Carbohydrates – 2 g

Fiber – 0.9 g

Fat – 0 g

Protein – 0.5 g

Calories – 10

Ingredients:

- 1 cup dried beans, of choice
- ½ tsp sea salt

Instructions:

1. Rinse and soak the beans overnight in water and the sea salt.
2. In the morning, drain the beans and rinse them in a colander. Cover the beans until the next rinse.
3. Rinse and drain the beans several times a day until the beans begin to sprout. This should take 3 to 4 days, depending on the type of bean.
4. Keep refrigerated for a day or two.

DESSERTS

Coconut Ice Cream Sundae

Prep time: 5 minutes

Cooking time: 0 minutes

Servings: 4

Nutrients per serving:

Carbohydrates – 30.8 g

Fiber – 2.6 g

Fat – 22.7 g

Protein – 2.2 g

Calories – 306

Ingredients:

- 2 13-oz cans full-fat unsweetened coconut milk
- 1 cup coconut sugar
- ⅛ tsp sea salt
- 1 vanilla bean, split lengthwise, deseeded
- Toppings of choice (bananas, shredded unsweetened coconut, chopped almonds, strawberries)

Instructions:

1. In a blender, mix together the coconut milk, coconut sugar, salt, and vanilla bean seeds. Transfer the mixture to a freezer-safe bowl. Freeze overnight.
2. Place two scoops of the ice cream in a small bowl. Garnish with your favorite alkaline-friendly toppings. Serve.

Warm Peach Cobbler

Prep time: 15 minutes

Cooking time: 15 minutes

Servings: 6

Nutrients per serving:

Carbohydrates – 20.8 g

Fiber – 5.8 g

Fat – 16.8 g

Protein – 6.6. g

Calories – 240

Ingredients:

- 2 pounds peaches, peeled and roughly chopped
- 1 packet stevia
- 1 vanilla bean, split lengthwise, deseeded
- ¼ tsp cinnamon
- 1½ cups raw almonds
- ½ cup shredded unsweetened coconut
- 1 Tbsp coconut oil, melted
- ¼ tsp sea salt

Instructions:

1. Preheat oven to 350°F.
2. Spray a baking dish with cooking spray.
3. In a large saucepan over medium heat, combine the peaches, stevia, vanilla bean, and cinnamon. Bring to boil. Remove from heat.
4. In a food processor, pulse the almonds, coconut, coconut oil, and salt.
5. Place the peaches in the prepared baking dish. Top with the almond-coconut mixture.
6. Bake for 15 minutes, or until the top is lightly golden. Serve warm.

Thanksgiving Pudding

Prep time: 10 minutes
Cooking time: 1 hour
Servings: 8

Nutrients per serving:

Carbohydrates – 16.1 g
Fiber – 2.2 g
Fat – 0.6 g
Protein – 1.4 g
Calories – 69

Ingredients:

- 1 15-oz can unsweetened pumpkin purée
- ½ cup unsweetened coconut milk
- 1 tsp cinnamon
- ½ tsp nutmeg
- ¼ tsp sea salt
- ½ cup raisins
- ½ cup apples, peeled, cored, diced

Instructions:

1. Preheat oven to 350°F.
2. In a food processor, blend the pumpkin, coconut milk, cinnamon, nutmeg, and salt until aerated.
3. Add the raisins and apples. Pulse to combine. Pour the mixture into a 9-inch baking dish.
4. Bake in the preheated oven for 60 minutes, or until the top cracks slightly.
5. Serve warm.

Valentine's Day Dates

Prep time: 10 minutes

Cooking time: 0 minutes

Servings: 1

Nutrients per serving:

Carbohydrates – 27.5 g

Fiber – 4.3 g

Fat – 8 g

Protein – 2 g

Calories – 178

Ingredients:

- 4 pitted Medjool dates
- 4 almond halves, divided
- ¼ cup shredded unsweetened coconut

Instructions:

1. Slice the dates lengthwise without cutting all the way through, so the halves are still connected.
2. Press open the dates and lay them on a flat surface. Place one almond half on one side of a date. Fold the other side over to enclose the almond between the date halves. Repeat with remaining dates and almonds.
3. Put some coconut inside the date. Serve.

Melon Madness

Prep time: 15 minutes

Cooking time: 0 minutes

Servings: 4

Nutrients per serving:

Carbohydrates – 7.4 g

Fiber – 0.7 g

Fat – 0.2 g

Protein – 0.8 g

Calories – 31

Ingredients:

- ½ watermelon, cut lengthwise, flesh scooped into balls, shell reserved
- 1 cup bite-size honeydew melon pieces
- 1 cup bite-size cantaloupe pieces

Instructions:

1. In a large bowl, combine the watermelon balls, honeydew, and cantaloupe.
2. Transfer the fruit to the watermelon shell and serve.

Summer Fruit Crisp

Prep time: 15 minutes

Cooking time: 15 minutes

Servings: 6

Nutrients per serving:

Carbohydrates – 20.8 g

Fiber – 5.8 g

Fat – 16.8 g

Protein – 6.6 g

Calories – 240

Ingredients:

- 2 cups chopped summer fruits, like strawberries and plums
- 1 packet stevia
- 1 vanilla bean, split lengthwise, deseeded
- 1½ cups raw almonds
- ½ cup shredded unsweetened coconut
- 1 Tbsp coconut oil, melted
- ¼ tsp sea salt

Instructions:

1. Preheat oven to 350°F.
2. Spray a baking dish with cooking spray.
3. In a large saucepan over medium heat, combine fruits, stevia, and vanilla bean seeds. Remove from the heat.
4. In a food processor, mix the almonds, coconut, coconut oil, and salt. Pulse until a sticky, crumbly mixture forms.
5. Transfer fruits to the prepared baking dish. Top with the almond-coconut mixture.
6. Bake for 15 minutes, or until the top is lightly golden.
7. Serve warm.

Summer Afternoon Ice Pops

Prep time: 2 hours 5 minutes

Cooking time: 0 minutes

Servings: 6

Nutrients per serving:

Carbohydrates – 7.1 g

Fiber – 4.2 g

Fat – 14.1 g

Protein – 2.5 g

Calories – 163

Ingredients:

- 1 13-oz can unsweetened coconut milk
- 1 packet stevia
- 1 vanilla bean, split lengthwise, deseed
- 1½ cups fresh fruit, chopped

Instructions:

1. In a bowl, mix together the coconut milk, stevia, and vanilla bean seeds.
2. Evenly divide the chopped fruit among the ice pop molds.
3. Pour the coconut milk mixture over the fruit, gently shaking each mold to settle the milk.
4. Insert ice pop handles into the molds. Freeze until completely frozen, about 2 hours.

No-Bake Fig Newtons

Prep time: 15 minutes

Cooking time: 0 minutes

Servings: 12

Nutrients per serving:

Carbohydrates – 32.3 g

Fiber – 5.1 g

Fat – 4.4 g

Protein – 3.6 g

Calories – 170

Ingredients:

- 3 cups dried figs, stemmed
- 1 cup raw almonds
- 1 vanilla bean, split lengthwise, deseeded
- ½ tsp sea salt

Instructions:

1. In a food processor, combine all ingredients. Pulse until a dough forms.
2. Scoop the dough by tablespoon and roll into balls by hand.
3. Keep refrigerated in an airtight container for one week.

SMOOTHIES

Tropical Pina Colada Smoothie

Prep time: 2 minutes

Cooking time: 0 minutes

Servings: 1

Nutrients per serving:

Carbohydrates – 38.9 g

Fiber – 3.8 g

Fat – 3.2 g

Protein – 1.7 g

Calories – 175

Ingredients:

- ½ cup unsweetened coconut milk
- 2½ cups fresh pineapple chunks
- 1 cup ice cubes

Instructions:

1. Add all ingredients to a blender.
2. Blend until smooth.
3. Divide into two portions and serve.

Banana Nut Bread Smoothie

Prep time: 2 minutes

Cooking time: 0 minutes

Servings: 1

Nutrients per serving:

Carbohydrates – 33.4 g

Fiber – 7.2 g

Fat – 12.1 g

Protein – 6.3 g

Calories – 254

Ingredients:

- 1 cup filtered water
- 1 medium banana, peeled
- ¼ cup raw almonds
- ½ tsp cinnamon
- ¼ tsp nutmeg
- 1 whole vanilla bean, split lengthwise, deseeded
- ½ cup ice cubes

Instructions:

1. Combine all ingredients in a blender.
2. Blend until smooth.
3. Serve in a tall glass.

Orange Healthy Smoothie

Prep time: 2 minutes

Cooking time: 0 minutes

Servings: 1

Nutrients per serving:

Carbohydrates – 44 g

Fiber – 3.8 g

Fat –0.3 g

Protein – 2.3 g

Calories – 182

Ingredients:

- 6 ounces freshly squeezed orange juice
- 1 ounce unsweetened coconut milk
- 1 medium frozen banana, cut into chunks
- 1 vanilla bean, split lengthwise, deseeded
- 1 packet stevia

Instructions:

1. In a blender, combine all ingredients.
2. Process until smooth.
3. Serve in a tall glass.

Mango, Papaya, Raspberry Smoothie

Prep time: 2 minutes

Cooking time: 0 minutes

Servings: 1

Nutrients per serving:

Carbohydrates – 39.7 g

Fiber – 6.7 g

Fat –0.06 g

Protein – 2.1 g

Calories – 153

Ingredients:

- ¼ cup raspberries
- ¾ cup frozen mango pieces
- ½ medium papaya, seeds removed, chopped

Instructions:

1. In a blender, combine all ingredients.
2. Process until smooth.
3. Serve in a tall glass.

Pumpkin Drink

Prep time: 2 minutes

Cooking time: 0 minutes

Servings: 1

Nutrients per serving:

Carbohydrates – 47.6 g

Fiber – 7.6 g

Fat – 5.5 g

Protein – 3.6 g

Calories – 240

Ingredients:

- ½ cup pumpkin purée
- 1 banana, frozen
- 1 cup unsweetened coconut milk
- 1 vanilla bean, split lengthwise, deseeded
- ¼ tsp cinnamon
- ⅛ tsp nutmeg
- ⅛ tsp allspice
- ½ cup ice cubes

Instructions:

1. In a blender, combine all ingredients.
2. Process until smooth.
3. Serve in a tall glass.

Basic Green Smoothie

Prep time: 2 minutes

Cooking time: 0 minutes

Servings: 1

Nutrients per serving:

Carbohydrates – 43.5 g

Fiber – 5.8 g

Fat – 6 g

Protein – 4.9 g

Calories – 230

Ingredients:

- 1 cup spinach
- 1 cup unsweetened coconut milk
- 1 cup frozen sliced peaches

Instructions:

1. In a blender, combine all ingredients.
2. Process until smooth.
3. Serve in a tall glass.

More-Than-a-Mojito Smoothie

Prep time: 2 minutes

Cooking time: 0 minutes

Servings: 1

Nutrients per serving:

Carbohydrates – 60.4 g

Fiber – 5.3 g

Fat –1.5 g

Protein – 2.6 g

Calories – 241

Ingredients:

- 1 cup spinach
- 1 cup unsweetened coconut water
- 2 cups pineapple
- 2 Tbsp fresh mint leaves
- Juice of ½ lime

Instructions:

1. In a blender, combine all ingredients.
2. Process until smooth.
3. Serve in a tall glass.

Avocado & Spinach Smoothie

Prep time: 2 minutes

Cooking time: 0 minutes

Servings: 1

Nutrients per serving:

Carbohydrates – 24.8 g

Fiber – 9.5 g

Fat –20.1 g

Protein – 5.6 g

Calories – 274

Ingredients:

- ½ avocado
- 1 cup spinach
- ¼ cup cilantro
- 1 cup fresh tomato juice
- Pinch garlic powder
- Pinch sea salt
- Pinch cayenne pepper
- ½ cup cherry tomatoes
- ½ cup diced cucumber

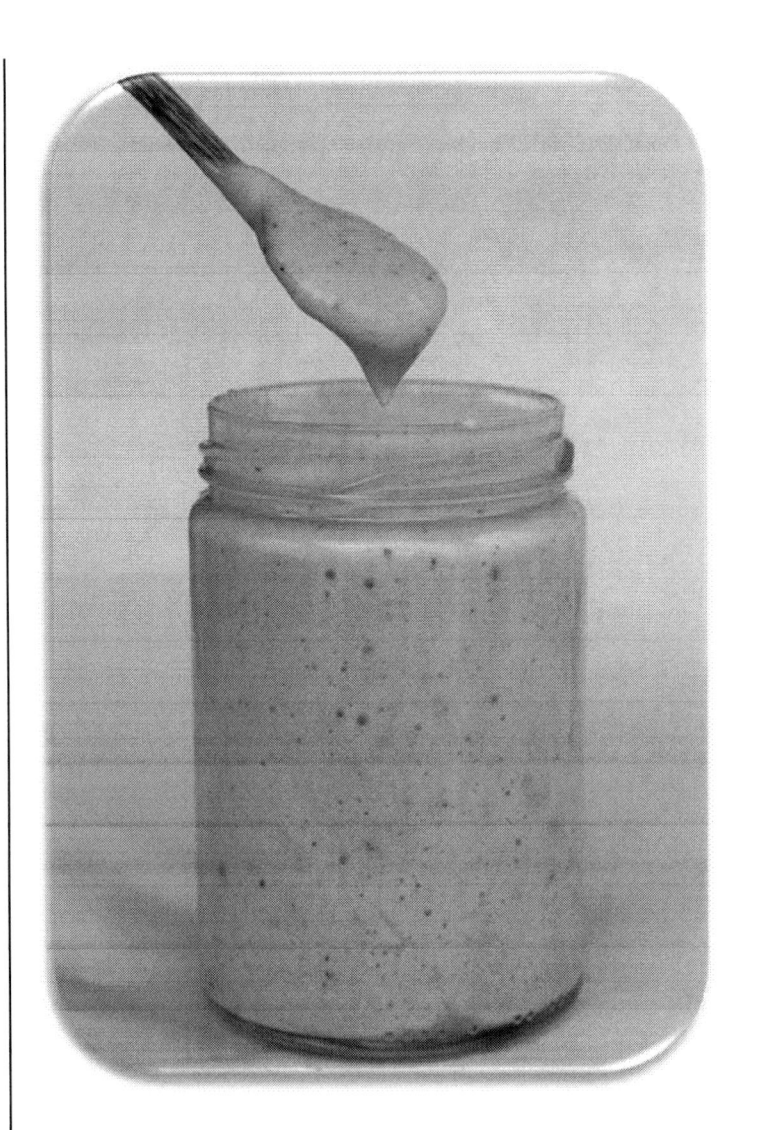

Instructions:

1. In a blender, add the avocado, spinach, cilantro, tomato juice, garlic powder, salt, and cayenne.
2. Blend until smooth.
3. Add the cherry tomatoes and cucumber, and blend until small chunks remain.
4. Store in an airtight container.

Orange, Peach, Kale Smoothie

Prep time: 10 minutes

Cooking time: 0 minutes

Servings: 1

Nutrients per serving:

Carbohydrates – 38 g

Fiber – 6.9 g

Fat –0.05 g

Protein – 4.6 g

Calories – 158

Ingredients:

- 1 orange, peeled, seeded
- 1 medium peach, peeled, sliced
- 1 cup kale, chopped
- 8 ounces filtered water

Instructions:

1. In a blender, combine all ingredients.
2. Process until smooth.
3. Serve in a tall glass.

CONDIMENTS, SAUCES & DRESSINGS

Homemade Ketchup

Prep time: 5 minutes

Cooking time: 10 minutes

Servings: 2

Nutrients per serving:

Carbohydrates – 38.5 g

Fiber – 2.7 g

Fat – 3.5 g

Protein – 11.7 g

Calories – 172

Ingredients:

- 1 6-oz can unsweetened tomato paste
- ½ cup brown rice syrup
- ½ cup apple cider vinegar
- 1 packet stevia
- ¼ tsp onion powder
- ⅛ tsp garlic powder

Instructions:

1. In a saucepan over medium heat, combine all ingredients. Whisk until smooth.
2. Bring the mixture to a boil. Then simmer for 25 minutes, stirring frequently.
3. Chill and serve cold.

Salsa Fresca

Prep time: 20 minutes

Cooking time: 0 minutes

Servings: 6

Nutrients per serving:

Carbohydrates – 4.6 g

Fiber – 1.2 g

Fat – 0.4 g

Protein – 1.5 g

Calories – 25

Ingredients:

- 4 fully ripened tomatoes, diced
- ½ sweet onion , diced
- 1 tbsp cumin seeds, toasted
- ¼ cup fresh cilantro, chopped
- ¼ cup apple cider vinegar
- ½ tsp sea salt

Instructions:

1. In a large airtight container, mix together all ingredients.
2. Cover and chill for 15 minutes, so the flavors blend before serving.

Hawaiian Salsa

Prep time: 20 minutes

Cooking time: 0 minutes

Servings: 6

Nutrients per serving:

Carbohydrates – 5.3 g

Fiber – 1.4 g

Fat – 0.2 g

Protein – 0.9 g

Calories – 48

Ingredients:

- 4 fully ripened tomatoes, diced
- ½ sweet onion, diced
- ½ cup fresh mango, diced
- ½ cup pineapple, diced
- ¼ cup apple cider vinegar
- ½ tsp sea salt

Instructions:

1. In a large airtight container, mix together all ingredients.
2. Cover and chill for 15 minutes so the flavors blend before serving.

Great Gravy

Prep time: 5 minutes

Cooking time: 10 minutes

Servings: 6

Nutrients per serving:

Carbohydrates – 2.8 g

Fiber – 0.8 g

Fat – 2.5 g

Protein – 1.8 g

Calories – 35

Ingredients:

- 1 Tbsp coconut oil, melted
- 2 Tbsp coconut flour
- ½ cup vegetable broth
- 2 Tbsp almond milk
- ½ tsp sea salt

Instructions:

1. In a saucepan over medium heat, heat the coconut oil. Don't let it get too hot or the flour will instantly burn.
2. Add the coconut flour and whisk to make a thick paste.
3. Slowly whisk in the vegetable broth. Bring to a boil and cook for 4 minutes, or until thickened.
4. Reduce the heat to low. Add the almond milk and salt. Continue cooking until the desired consistency.
5. Serve warm.

Apple Butter

Prep time: 10 minutes

Cooking time: 3 hours

Servings: 24

Nutrients per serving:

Carbohydrates – 12.9 g

Fiber – 1.9 g

Fat – 0.2 g

Protein – 0.2 g

Calories – 49

Ingredients:

- 4 pounds apples, peeled, chopped
- 2 cups fresh apple juice
- 1 Tbsp lemon juice, freshly squeezed
- 2 packets stevia
- 1 tsp cinnamon
- 1 vanilla bean, split lengthwise, deseeded
- Pinch ground cloves

Instructions:

1. Add the apples, apple juice, and lemon juice to a pot. Bring to a simmer and cook for 1 hour, until soft. Remove from the heat and cool slightly.
2. In a blender, purée the apples until smooth.
3. Take the puree out. Add the stevia, cinnamon, vanilla bean seeds, and cloves to the apples. Cook for an additional 2 hours, stirring frequently.
4. Cool the apple butter. Transfer to an airtight container and refrigerate.

Sun-Dried Tomato Sauce

Prep time: 10 minutes

Cooking time: 0 minutes

Servings: 4

Nutrients per serving:

Carbohydrates – 6.1 g

Fiber – 1.5 g

Fat – 12.2 g

Protein – 1.4 g

Calories – 132

Ingredients:

- 1 cup cherry tomatoes, halved
- ½ cup tightly packed sun-dried tomatoes
- 3 Tbsp coconut oil
- 1/3 cup fresh basil
- 1 Tbsp tomato paste
- 1 tsp sea salt
- 1 tsp garlic powder

Instructions:

1. In a food processor, combine all ingredients.
2. Pulse to combine.

Enchilada Sauce

Prep time: 5 minutes

Cooking time: 26 minutes

Servings: 8

Nutrients per serving:

Carbohydrates – 8.3 g

Fiber – 1.6 g

Fat – 3.6 g

Protein – 1.8 g

Calories – 68

Ingredients:

- 2 Tbsp coconut oil
- 2 Tbsp coconut flour
- 2 Tbsp chili powder
- 2 cups water
- 1 8-oz can tomato paste
- 1 tsp garlic powder
- ½ tsp cumin
- ½ tsp onion powder
- ½ tsp sea salt
- ¼ tsp red pepper flakes

Instructions:

1. In a pot over medium heat, heat the coconut oil, coconut flour, and chili powder. Cook for 1 minute.
2. Add the water, tomato paste, garlic powder, cumin, onion powder, salt, and red pepper flakes, to taste. Bring the mixture to a simmer and cook for 25 minutes, stirring occasionally.
3. Serve warm.

CONCLUSION

Thank you for reading this book and having the patience to try the recipes.

I do hope that you gain as much enjoyment reading and experimenting with the meals as I have had writing this book.

If you would like to leave a comment, you can do it at the Order section->Digital orders, in your amazon account.

Stay safe and healthy!

Recipe Index

A
All-American Apple Pie 26
Angel Hair Pasta with Tomato Sause 51
Apple Butter 82
Avocado & Spinach Smoothie 76
Avocado-Caprese Salad 38

B
Baby Potato Home Fries 27
Banana Nut Bread Smoothie 70
Basic Green Smoothie 74
BBB Soup 57
Better than Chicken Soup 50
Breakfast Fajitas 28
Brown Rice Porridge 29

C
Championship Chili 54
Coconut Ice Cream Sundae 61
Curried Eggplant 53

D
Date Night Broccoli Bake 55

E
Emeraland Forest Salad 34
Enchilada Sauce 84

G
Garden Pancakes 22
Good Morning Popeye 21
Great Gravy 81
Grilled Vegetables Stack 58

H
Hawaiian Salsa 80
Homemade Ketchup 78

M
Mango, Papaya, Raspberry Smoothie 72
Melon Madness 65
More-Than-a-Mojito Smoothie 75

N
No BS Brussels Sprouts 59
No-Bake Fig Newtons 68

O
Orange Healthy Smoothie 71
Orange, Peach, Kale Smoothie 77
Organic Baby Tomato & Kale Salad 40

P
Pumpkin Drink 73

Q
Quinoa & Avocado Salad 37

R
Roasted Vegetable Salad 36

S
Salad in Your Hand 31
Salad on a Stick 33
Salsa Fresca 79
Spaghetti Squash Hash Browns 30
Spicy Sesame Noodle Salad 39
Sprouted Beans 60
Stuffed Peppers 52
Summer Afternoon Ice Pops 67
Summer Dinner Salad 35
Summer Fruit Crisp 66
Summer Fruit Salad with Lime & Mint 24
Sun-Dried Tomato Sauce 83

T
Thanksgiving Anytime Roasted Vegetables .. 56
Thanksgiving Pudding 63
The Asian Bowl 41
The Breakup Bowl 42
The Fight It Off Bowl 43
The Hawaiian Bowl 44
The Indian Bowl 45
The Italian Bowl 46
The Mexican Bowl 47
The Rose Bowl 48
The Southern Bowl 49
Tropical Granola 23
Tropical Pina Colada Smoothie 69

V
Valentine`s Day Dates 64

W
Warm Peach Cobbler 62
Warm Spinach Salad 32
Winter Fruit Compote with Figs & Ginger ... 25

Conversion Tables

VALUME EQUIVALENTS (LIQUID)

US STANDARD	US STANDARD (OUNCES)	METRIC (% PROXIMATE)
2 tablespoons	1 fl. oz.	30 mL
¼ cup	2 fl. oz.	60 mL
½ cup	4 fl. oz.	120 mL
1 cup	8 fl. oz.	240 mL
1 ½ cup	12 fl. oz.	355 mL
2 cups or 1 pint	16 fl. oz.	475 mL
4 cups or 1 quart	32 fl. oz.	1 L
1 gallon	128 fl. oz.	4 L

OVEN TEMPERATURES

FAHRENHEIT(F)	CELSIUS(C) APPROXIMATE
250 °F	120 °C
300 °F	150 °C
325 °F	165 °C
350 °F	180 °C
375 °F	190 °C
400 °F	200 °C
425 °F	220 °C
450 °F	230 °C

VALUME EQUIVALENTS (LIQUID)

US STANDARD	METRIC (APPROXIMATE)
1/8 teaspoon	0.5 mL
¼ teaspoon	1 mL
½ teaspoon	2 mL
2/3 teaspoon	4 mL
1 teaspoon	5 mL
1 tablespoon	15 mL
¼ cup	59 mL
1/3 cup	79 mL
½ cup	118 mL
2/3 cup	156 mL
¾ cup	177 mL
1 cup	235 mL
2 cups or 1 pint	475 mL
3 cups	700 mL
4 cups or 1 quart	1 L
½ gallon	2 L
1 gallon	4 L

WEIGHT EQUIVALENTS

US STANDARD	METRIC (APPROXIMATE)
½ ounce	15 g
1 ounces	30 g
2 ounces	60 g
4 ounces	115 g
8 ounces	225 g
12 ounces	340 g
16 ounce or 1 pound	455 g

Other Books by Emma Green

Intermittent Fasting https://goo.gl/i4WMva

South Beach Diet https://goo.gl/BKysXU

Meal Prep https://goo.gl/N8f9XU

Anti-Inflammatori Diet https://goo.gl/EW9nqc

Made in the USA
Middletown, DE
05 January 2019